Highwaymen and Brigands

Macdonald Educational

Robin Hood

Nobody knows who Robin Hood really was, or even if he was a real person. Some people think that all the stories and songs about outlaws in the Middle Ages became connected with just one outlaw as they were told over and over again. The outlaw was called Robin Hood because that name was so common in the Middle Ages. So, the Robin Hood legend was born.

Robin Hood is said to have been a noble outlaw who stole from the rich and gave to the poor. Many stories say that he and his band, which included Little John, Much the Miller, Will Scarlet and Friar Tuck, lived in Sherwood Forest, near Nottingham. These men were very loyal to one another.

Usually Robin Hood would send out his men to ambush a rich knight or landowner travelling through the forest and bring him back to the outlaws' hideout. There the captive would be invited to sit down for a feast. Robin Hood was a polite robber! After the meal he would ask the captive to pay handsomely for his food—which sometimes meant all the money the man had—and then let him go. If the band brought back a man who was in trouble, Robin Hood might lend him money or help him fight his enemies.

Robin Hood was also known as an expert shot with his bow and arrow. Sometimes he ventured out of the forest to take part in archery contests which he always won.

Robin Hood has become many people's idea of the perfect outlaw who robbed only the rich and was kind to the less fortunate. Most real outlaws, though, were not so noble, as we shall see.

Moll Cutpurse

Moll Cutpurse was a highwaywoman who managed to make more money than most highwaymen. She operated in and around London.

Besides being a successful robber, Moll received stolen goods from other thieves which she then sold. When wealthy people had their watches or jewels stolen, they knew that sooner or later their property would end up with Moll. They would go to her and buy it back. Moll made so much money that whenever she was arrested she could bribe the constables to set her free. So instead of being hanged, she lived to the age of 75.

Moll, whose real name was Mary Frith, was brought up like most little girls in the 16th century. But she refused to wear women's clothing and preferred to play and fight with boys. She was big and strong, and later when she became a highway robber, she had no trouble disguising herself as a man. We know that her father was a shoemaker and her uncle was a minister!

Moll's fame soon spread far and wide. There was even a play written about her when she was only 26. It was called "The Roaring Girle" because she had such a powerful voice.

People often made fun of Moll. Once she went to a grocer's stall in the market to have a pipeful of tobacco. The grocer's boy gave her a pipe filled with gunpowder instead. When Moll lit it, it exploded in her face! Moll was furious. She threw the pipe at the boy's head, and threatened to blow up the boy and his master with what she called "engines and devices". But we do not know whether she kept her word.

After Him!

Said a black-hearted brigand from Bree,
"A collector of taxes, that's me!
By robbing the great,
I am serving the state—
And I don't even charge any fee!"

Card Film

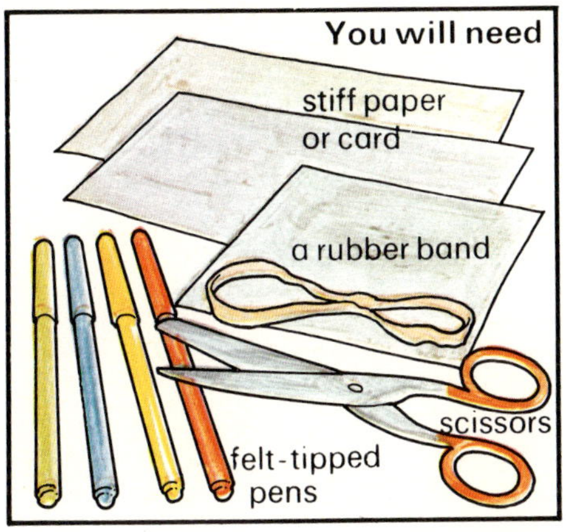

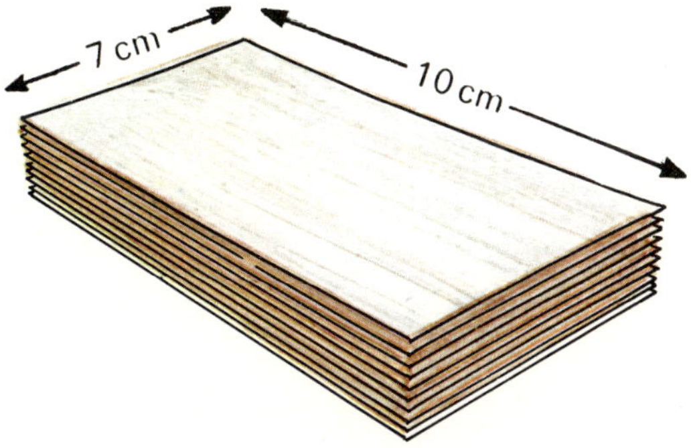

1. Cut your card or paper into 10 pieces of the same size, 10 × 7 cm.

2. Think of an action to show in your film. You could show a highwayman riding his horse or Robin Hood shooting an arrow.

Draw a picture on the right half of one side of each card. Each picture must be a little different so when you flip the cards they will look like a film.

3. Draw on one half of the card.

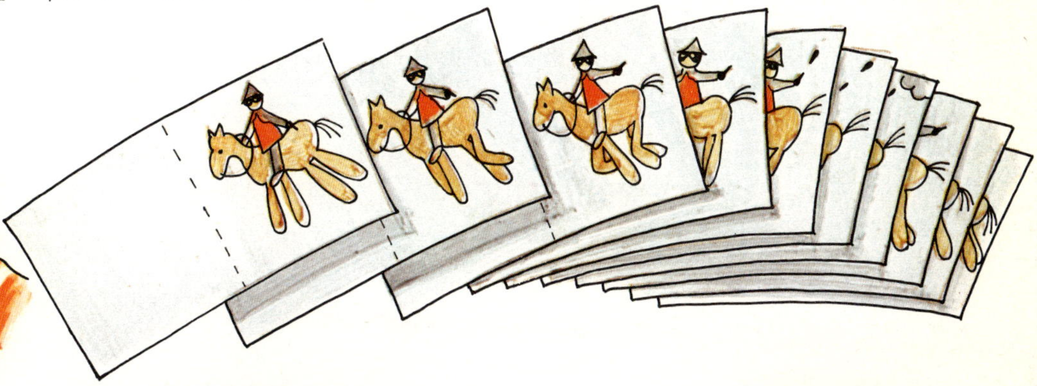

4. Each picture is a little different.

5. Put the cards together in order. Put a rubber band around them.

6. On the other side you can make another film.

7. Flip the cards quickly with your thumb and see your card film.

William Davis

William Davis was a prosperous farmer in the 17th century. He was known as "The Golden Farmer" because he always paid for everything in gold.

Little did his friends or even his family know that he spent his evenings robbing people on the highway. But instead of using the stolen goods to pay his debts, he first sold them for gold with which he paid his bills.

By day he managed his farm and was a respected gentleman. By night he roamed the roads of Surrey, not caring whether he robbed the rich or the poor. He was just as likely to take a few pounds from a poor tinker as three gold and diamond rings from a Duchess, having first shot her footmen and coachman. It is said that once Davis even stole back the money he had paid as rent to the man who owned his farm. Davis first paid his landlord and then, in disguise, rode after the man and stole all his money at gunpoint.

Davis was clever and lucky. He had an unusually long career on the highway and then he retired.

But after a few years he began to rob again, in hopes of making enough money to buy some land and so enlarge his farm.

Perhaps because he was growing old or was simply out of practice, he was recognised during an attempted holdup and captured.

He was tried, condemned and hanged in 1690 at the age of 64. His body was hung in chains on Bagshot Heath to warn other highwaymen of the fate that lay in store for them. Most, however, did not survive half as long as Davis.

How Robin Hood Feasted the Sheriff

A comedy, with:
The Sheriff of Nottingham
Robin Hood
Will Scarlet
Alan-a-Dale
Friar Tuck
Little John
Maid Marian
The six daughters of Sir Richard at the Lee
Much the Miller
A cook
Five archers

(Scene: a clearing in the Forest of Sherwood. The Sheriff enters)

Sheriff I am the Sheriff of Nottingham Town, and a mighty man am I!
(Three notes on a horn are heard. Robin enters)

Robin And I am Robin of Sherwood Forest. Surrender yourself to me!

Sheriff Never! I shall fight you! I shall defeat you! Where are my men?

Robin They are fled.

Sheriff *(Falls to his knees)* Help! Mercy, bold Robin, mercy!

Robin On your feet, you black-hearted rogue! We have plans for you. *(Calling)* Will Scarlet and Alan-a-Dale! Friar Tuck and Little John!
(They enter, each answering "Here, Robin!")

Will So—the Sheriff of Nottingham rode into the forest!

Alan With all his men?

Tuck But they ran away from the men in Lincoln green!

Little John Leaving their master begging for mercy!

Robin On his knees! Up, you villain!

Sheriff Help! Mercy, Robin! Mercy!

Robin Mercy? Did you show mercy to my good friend, Sir Richard at the Lee, when you put him in the dungeon of Nottingham Castle?

Sheriff Sir Richard owes me money.

Will Only for taxes you had no right to demand.

Alan You owe Sir Richard money!

Tuck For taxes he has already paid.

Little John So, now, you will release him, and then you will repay him.

Sheriff Never! Oh, no! Oh, dear me, no!

Robin We shall see. Will Scarlet! Call Maid Marian and the six daughters of poor Sir Richard.

Will *(Calling)* Lady Marian! Bring the daughters of Sir Richard to meet the villain who has imprisoned their father!

Alan The Lady Marian and the daughters of Sir Richard plan to make a fine feast for you, Master Sheriff.

Sheriff A feast? What do you mean? What are you up to?

Tuck We know you like to eat well, Sir Sheriff. We thought a feast would be a proper thing for such an honoured guest!

Sheriff This is a trick!

Little John And a very pretty one, too!

Sheriff You will not force *me* to eat the rubbish you outlaws live on. Never!
(Maid Marian and the six daughters of Sir Richard at the Lee enter)

Marian Of course not, Sheriff! Robin sent one of his band into Nottingham to bring back food and dishes of the very best.

Daughter 1 Yes, Sheriff, Much the Miller has gone shopping!

Daughter 2 Yes, he has gone to Nottingham, Sheriff.

Daughter 3 In Nottingham Town he will get us the finest food.

Daughter 4 And he will bring back the costliest dishes to eat it from.

Daughter 5 Everything in his basket will be fit for a king!

Daughter 6 Or a very fat Sheriff!

Marian So you see how we honour you, Sheriff?

Sheriff You are up to something!

Robin Of course we are, Sheriff! We plan to offer you a feast to remember!

Will With everything cooked just as you like it!

Alan We will give you the rarest of wines!

Tuck And we will entertain you like a prince!

Little John You will be grateful, Sheriff—you will be *so* grateful!

Marian Oh, Sheriff, you *will* be grateful!

Daughters And then you will let our father go!

Sheriff Grateful? Never! Let him go? Never!
(A horn is heard)

by Richard Blythe

Robin Listen! There is the horn of Much the Miller. He has returned from Nottingham. He is back from his shopping!

Will Stand the Sheriff by this tree.

Alan We don't want him to miss anything!

Tuck No, that would be a *great* pity!

Little John *(Calling)* Bring us your shopping, Much! We are ready for you!

(Much the Miller enters, with an archer who leads a frightened prisoner, the cook)

Much Bold Robin—here is the first thing I have brought back from Nottingham Town!

Sheriff How dare you! That is my cook—you have stolen my cook!

Robin We stole your cook from your own house!

Daughter 1 Because he knows which dishes you like best!

Marian Take the cook, and tell him to build a fire.

(The archer leads the cook away)

Much *(Clapping his hands)* And here is the second thing I brought back from Nottingham.

(An archer brings on a heavy basket, which he shows to the Sheriff)

Sheriff My silver plate! My knives and forks! My spoons! My silver dishes!

Marian And all from your own house, Sheriff.

Daughter 2 Because we want you to feel at home!

Daughter 3 Take the dishes and the knives and forks to the cook.

Much And now for the third thing I brought back from Nottingham.

(An archer enters with another basket)

Tuck *(Looking inside)* Well! Meat, and fish, and bread—and *cakes*!

Little John Much, you rascal, you have been stealing from the Sheriff's larder!

Will But only the best is good enough for our Sheriff!

Alan And where can the best be found?

Robin In the Sheriff's own larder, of course!

Daughter 4 Take the meat and the fish and the bread and the cakes to the cook.

Sheriff Oh, you thieves! You rogues. You have robbed me, you have robbed my house! By heavens, I'll make you pay—you'll pay for this!

Robin Pay! Of course—the feast must be paid for!

Much I did not forget, Robin. *(Calling)* Bring us the Sheriff's chests of gold and silver!

Sheriff Gold? Silver?

(Two archers enter, with chests under their arms)

My treasure chests! My money! You have stolen my money!

Daughter 5 But why not, Sheriff? The cook must be paid!

Daughter 6 How else will you pay for your share of our feast?

Robin And you will *need* money, Sheriff, to pay back what you owe to Sir Richard—when you have released him. Sign this paper!

Sheriff Certainly not! I shall sign nothing! What is it?

Robin Orders, to the jailer at Nottingham Castle—telling him to release Sir Richard at the Lee.

Sheriff Release him? I shall not sign. Never!

Will Beat his cook and share out his food!

Alan Break his dishes and bury his gold!

Tuck Throw the Sheriff in the river!

Little John Hand me my cudgel!

Sheriff Mercy! Mercy!

Robin That's better.

Marian Much better!

Sheriff What will happen if I refuse to sign those orders?

Much We shall go straight back to your house in Nottingham, and carry off the rest of your treasure.

Sheriff Ahhh! *(He stamps and rages)* I am lost! You have won, you rogues—you have won! I will sign the paper.

Robin Excellent! Will Scarlet, bring ink! Alan-a-Dale, bring a pen! Friar Tuck and Little John, guard the Sheriff! While the Lady Marian and the daughters of good Sir Richard keep an eye on the cook, Much and I will ride into Nottingham with the Sheriff's orders. Sir Richard shall be brought back from prison—to join us at our feast!

(Why not make up the next scene by yourselves? It could be about Robin and Much at Nottingham Castle and how they get past the guards and release Sir Richard by making the jailer obey the order signed by the Sheriff. Or your scene could show the feast in the greenwood, when Robin and Much bring Sir Richard from prison to meet his old enemy, the Sheriff, face to face.)

Claude Duval

Claude Duval was a Frenchman but he became the most famous highwayman in 17th-century England. He was very good looking and women found him very charming. In fact, some women even hoped that he would rob them, just so that they could meet him.

Duval came to England as a footman to an English nobleman. As he was already a clever liar and a cheat, it was easy for him to leave his job and live by crime.

He soon became known for his daring and gallant holdups. Many stories were told about him, usually showing him in a good light. Once he is said to have stopped a coach carrying a gentleman and a lady who he knew had £400 on them. The lady picked up a flute and began to play to show that she was not afraid. Duval took out his own flute and started to play too. He then asked the gentleman if he might dance with the lady.

The gentleman, of course, dared not refuse, so Duval and the lady danced on the heath. After the dancing Duval demanded that he be paid for his performance. The gentleman graciously handed over £100. Duval was so pleased with this quick payment that he allowed the gentleman to keep the remaining £300.

But another story shows a different and probably more truthful picture of Duval. He and his gang held up a coach carrying some women, one of whom was feeding a baby from a silver bottle. Seeing the glint of the silver, Duval did not hesitate to snatch the bottle from the baby's lips.

Duval was finally caught and arrested one evening when he was too drunk to escape. Before he was hanged, aged only 27, many women came to see him in prison, and even more came to watch his execution.

Dick Turpin

Dick Turpin was England's most famous highwayman. As a young man he worked as a butcher, stocking his shop with sheep stolen from neighbouring farms. His thieving was discovered, and he fled to another part of the country. Turpin then became a smuggler and later joined a violent gang that broke into houses. A newspaper in 1735 reported that on one raid Turpin threatened to push an old woman into the fire if she did not hand over her wealth. In another raid, the paper reported, the gang beat an old man and emptied a kettle of hot water over his head.

When Turpin left the gang, he moved on to highway robbery. It is said that the first person he tried to rob was another highwayman, Tom King. The two joined forces and made Epping Forest, near London, so dangerous that people were terrified to walk through it.

Dick Turpin chatted calmly with the exec
ladder and being hanged.

for half an hour before jumping off the

By this time many romantic stories were being told about Turpin. The stories said he was a dashing, gallant rogue. His faithful horse, Bess, was said to have carried him to York in a daring escape, but people did not tell this story until 100 years after Turpin's death. It was made popular in a 19th-century novel.

Actually, Dick Turpin was one of the most brutal and cruel men who ever roamed the highways. Far from being handsome, his face was marked from small pox, and he was short and squat.

After his arrest he lived in prison and showed no fear of the execution that awaited him. On the way to the gallows he stood in the cart and bowed to the many people who had come to watch him die. Except for a moment when his leg trembled as he mounted the gallows' ladder, he was cool and calm. Then he was hanged.

Goodies and Baddies

You might like to dress up as a bandit or a detective and play with your friends. You could act out some of the stories in this book.

You can be a mysterious highwayman, a noble bandit or a Wild West train robber. Or you could be a Bow Street Runner or Pinkerton detective and catch the bandits! Here are some ideas. Can you think of more?

With a cotton scarf or fabric square be a highwayman or a Wild West outlaw.

Or be a Pinkerton detective.

Make a highwayman's or Bow Street Runner's hat from 3 strips of painted card, stapled like this.

Make a highwayman's mask from paper and string.

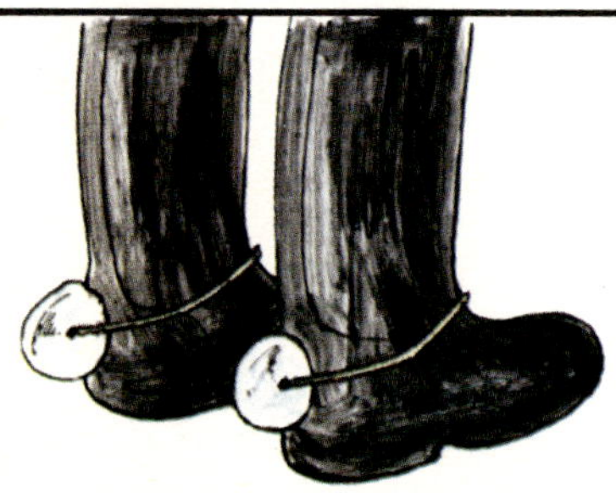

Punch holes in milk bottle tops. Put string through and tie around your wellies for spurs.

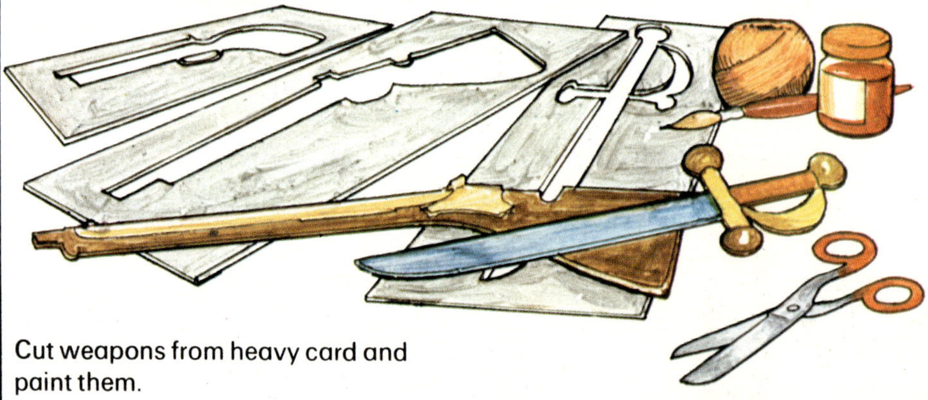

Cut weapons from heavy card and paint them.

Make Robin Hood's bow and arrows from sticks. Tie string across a long curved stick for the bow.

Make a quiver from rolled up coloured paper. Tape it and tie it on with string.

Only pretend to shoot your arrows. You could hurt someone if you really shot them.

Use a grown up's old shirt and a belt for a tunic.

Make a highwayman's cloak from a big piece of fabric or an old sheet or curtain. Tie it around your neck with ribbon.

The Highwayman by Alfred Noyes

The wind was a torrent of darkness among the gusty trees.
The moon was a ghostly galleon tossed upon cloudy seas.
The road was a ribbon of moonlight over the purple moor,
and the highwayman came riding—
        Riding—riding—
The highwayman came riding, up to the old inn-door.

He'd a French cocked-hat on his forehead, a bunch of lace at his chin,
A coat of the claret velvet, and breeches of brown doe-skin.
They fitted with never a wrinkle. His boots were up to the thigh.
And he rode with a jewelled twinkle,
        His pistol butts a-twinkle,
His rapier hilt a-twinkle, under the jewelled sky.

Over the cobbles he clattered and clashed in the dark inn-yard.
He tapped with his whip on the shutters, but all was locked and barred.
He whistled a tune to the window, and who should be waiting there
But the landlord's black-eyed daughter,
        Bess, the landlord's daughter,
Plaiting a dark red love-knot into her long black hair.

And dark in the dark old inn-yard a stable-wicket creaked
Where Tim the ostler listened. His face was white and peaked.
His eyes were hollows of madness, his hair like mouldy hay,
But he loved the landlord's daughter,
        The landlord's red-lipped daughter.
Dumb as a dog he listened, and he heard the robber say—

"One kiss, my bonny sweetheart, I'm after a prize to-night,
But I shall be back with the yellow gold before the morning light;
Yet, if they press me sharply, and harry me through the day,
Then look for me by moonlight,
        Watch for me by moonlight,
I'll come to thee by moonlight, though hell should bar the way."

He did not come in the dawning. He did not come at noon;
And out of the tawny sunset, before the rise of the moon,
When the road was a gypsy's ribbon, looping the purple moor,
A red-coat troop came marching—
        Marching—marching—
King George's men came marching, up to the old inn-door.

They said no word to the landlord. They drank his ale instead.
But they gagged his daughter, and bound her, to the foot of her narrow bed.
Two of them knelt at her casement, with muskets at their side!
There was death at every window;
        And hell at one dark window;
For Bess could see, through her casement, the road that *he* would ride.

They had tied her up to attention, with many a sniggering jest.
They had bound a musket beside her, with the muzzle beneath her breast!
"Now, keep good watch!" and they kissed her. She heard the doomed man say—
Look for me by moonlight;
Watch for me by moonlight;
I'll come to thee by moonlight, though hell should bar the way!

She twisted her hands behind her; but all the knots held good!
She writhed her hands till her fingers were wet with sweat or blood!
They stretched and strained in the darkness, and the hours crawled by like years,
Till, now, on the stroke of midnight,
Cold, on the stroke of midnight,
The tip of one finger touched it! The trigger at least was hers!

Tlot-tlot; tlot-tlot! Had they heard it? The horsehoofs ringing clear;
Tlot-tlot, tlot-tlot, in the distance? Were they deaf that they did not hear?
Down the ribbon of moonlight, over the brow of the hill,
The highwayman came riding—
Riding—riding—
The red-coats looked to their priming! She stood up, straight and still.

Tlot-tlot, in the frosty silence! *Tlot-tlot*, in the echoing night!
Nearer he came and nearer. Her face was like a light.
Her eyes grew wide for a moment; she drew one last deep breath,
Then her finger moved in the moonlight,
Her musket shattered the moonlight,
Shattered her breast in the moonlight and warned him—with her death.

He turned. He spurred to the west; he did not know who stood
Bowed, with her head o'er the musket, drenched with her own blood!
Not till the dawn he heard it, and his face grew grey to hear
How Bess, the landlord's daughter,
The landlord's black-eyed daughter,
Had watched for her love in the moonlight, and died in the darkness there.

Back, he spurred like a madman, shouting a curse to the sky,
With the white road smoking behind him and his rapier brandished high.
Blood-red were his spurs in the golden moon; wine-red was his velvet coat;
When they shot him down on the highway,
Down like a dog on the highway,
And he lay in his blood on the highway, with a bunch of lace at his throat.

Don José

Don José was a Spanish bandit in the 19th century. A famous short story and a great opera were written about him and Carmen, the Gypsy woman he loved.

In the story Don José first met Carmen when he was a soldier guarding a factory. Carmen was young, very beautiful and quick-tempered. She had slashed the face of another woman while they were working and was to be taken to prison. Carmen asked Don José to help her escape. She succeeded, but Don José was imprisoned for helping her.

Carmen sent Don José a loaf of bread with an iron file baked inside it so he could file away the bars of his cell. He was too proud to attempt an escape, but he loved Carmen all the more because she had tried to help him.

When Don José came out of prison, he found Carmen again. She suggested that he join her bandit friends in the mountains. Don José agreed and became an outlaw.

Carmen would often lure rich men into the mountains where the bandits would be waiting to ambush their coaches. Once she went to the city and met a rich Englishman. She pretended to be in love with him, and he invited her on a journey. Carmen then told Don José just where their coach was going so the bandits could lie in wait for it. When the coach came to the hideout, the bandits attacked it. The Englishman was skilful with a pistol and would have shot Don José, but Carmen pushed his arm so he missed.

After a time Carmen got tired of Don José and wanted to go off with another man. Don José begged her to stay. He asked her to go to America with him and begin a new life, but Carmen would not come. Don José was so angry that he murdered her. He was thrown into prison. Later the King of Spain pardoned him.

Shoebox Theatre

You will need

1. Ask a grown up to cut out the sides of a shoebox like this.

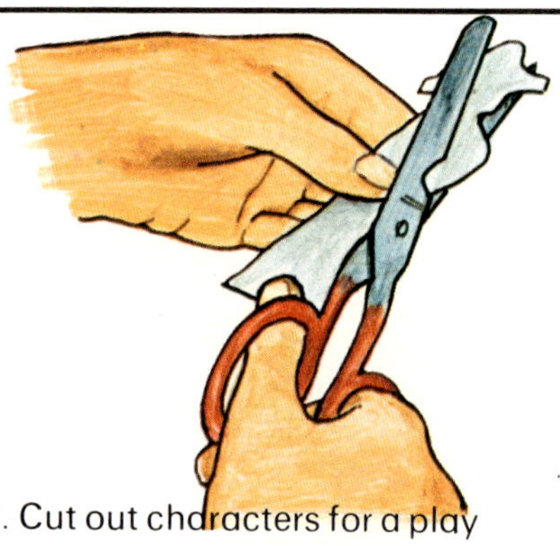

2. Cut out characters for a play from card.

3. Draw in clothing, faces and hair with felt-tipped pens.

You can draw horses and coaches too.

4. Tape the figures to the ends of long pencils.

5. You can push the pencils through the slits in the box to make the characters act a play.

6. For scenery, cut a piece of card so it is the same length as the box.

You could make up a play about one of the outlaws in this book, or act out the play on page 12. Make all the characters and scenery you need and put on a performance for your friends.

7. Draw scenery on the card.

8. Put the scenery in the back of the box. You can have new scenery for each scene in the play.

Sandor Rozsa

Sandor Rozsa was Hungary's most famous brigand. He lived in the 19th century, and his father was hanged for stealing horses.

When Rozsa was 22 he was caught stealing some cattle. He was sentenced to ten years in prison and a severe caning every three months. After ten months of hard labour, he and a friend managed to take off each other's chains and escape. Then Rozsa became a brigand, stealing and selling horses, with the police constantly at his heels. Rozsa was a noble robber. He rarely stole from poor people, and he always sided with the poor against the rich and powerful.

Many years later, even though Rozsa was accused of having killed two policemen and a chief constable, he asked the king for a pardon. This was refused and a new effort was made to arrest him. But there was no catching Rozsa. The peasants loved him and helped him to hide. They made up poems and songs about his valiant deeds.

Then Rozsa was told he would be pardoned if he agreed to fight in Hungary's war of independence against Austria. Rozsa gathered 80 men. Their job was to rob the enemy of cattle and horses. Then one day Rozsa saw an officer treating some peasants unjustly. In disgust he and his men quit the army.

Finally Rozsa was caught. He was hiding out in a haystack in a peasant's back yard. One day he thought the peasant had betrayed him. He went into the peasant's house and shot the man. The bullet hit the peasant in the arm. Hearing the noise, the peasant's wife and daughter rushed in. The wife hit Rozsa over the head with a frying pan. Rozsa was overpowered, handed over to the police and sent to prison. The peasant died from his wound.

Rozsa was later pardoned, but he took up horse thieving again. He was caught once more and died in prison in 1878 as an old man.

Thief-Takers

This game is for 2 or more players. You will need 1 or 2 dice, some counters and lots of milk bottle tops and beer bottle tops for money.

Each milk bottle top is worth £5, and each beer bottle top is worth £1. One player should be the banker. Each player receives 7 milk bottle tops and 5 beer bottle tops worth £40 before the game begins. The bank should have at least 17 milk bottle tops and 10 beer bottle tops worth £100 in it.

First take turns to throw the dice. The person who throws the highest number begins. Then each player throws in turn and moves his or her counter the number of places shown on the dice.

If you land on a square with instructions, you must follow them. Any money you win or lose must come out of or go into the bank.

The player who reaches the end first gets a £5 bonus, but the winner is the player who finishes with the most money.

1. START

2. You catch a thief who robbed the Prime Minister. Reward £20.

3.

4.

5. A fine lady pays you £5 to recover her stolen jewels.

6. Your horse is stolen. Buy a new one for £12.

7.

8. You are ambushed and left bound and gagged. Lose 1 turn.

9. GAMBLERS' TAVERN
If you throw an even number, receive that number of pounds, if an odd number, give that number of pounds.

10.

11. You guard a mailcoach on a journey. Wages £20.

12.

13. You are shadowing a brigand. Go back to Gamblers' Tavern, square 9.

14. Running from a band of thieves you drop £10.

15.

16.

You are
about a
hway-
n's
eout.
ve
other turn.

39. You help a friend to catch a thief. Reward £3.

40.

41. You bribe a gang of thieves to let you go. Lose £10.

42.

43. Sell your horse for £12 but miss 1 turn while walking.

44.

45. You frighten away thieves from a victim. Reward £10.

46. THE END
£5 bonus to the first.

The James Gang

Jesse James

Jesse and Frank James were rebel outlaws during the American civil war in the 1860's. After they returned from the war no one would give them jobs, and they needed money. They realised they could attack trains and towns and banks in peacetime, just as they had during the war.

The James gang made such swift getaways that at first no one knew for sure that they had even carried out certain robberies. But after they were identified, they were sometimes accused of two or more robberies that took place at the same time, many miles apart.

They were best known for robbing trains. They would pull a rail out of line so the approaching train would be derailed. Often the train would be badly damaged and passengers and crew hurt or killed. The gang then stole some of the cargo and robbed the passengers.

There were rewards totalling $3000 offered for the

arrest of Frank and Jesse, but no one could catch them. A group of bankers hired the famous Pinkerton's National Detective Agency to track them down. The Pinkerton agents surrounded the James's house and tossed a bomb in through the window. The explosion killed Jesse and Frank's 9-year-old brother, and their mother lost an arm. Jesse and Frank were not even in the house. Many people felt this was a cowardly attack and sided with the James brothers. Jesse and Frank became national heroes.

Later Jesse and Frank found new homes with their families and took new names. But they continued to rob. In 1882 a friend named Bob Ford came to visit Jesse. Ford had been offered $10,000 to shoot Jesse, and he did so. Ten years later Ford was shot by a friend of Jesse's. Frank James, afraid that he, too, would be shot, gave himself up. He was allowed to go free and lived to be an old man.

Frank James

The Jolly Highwayman

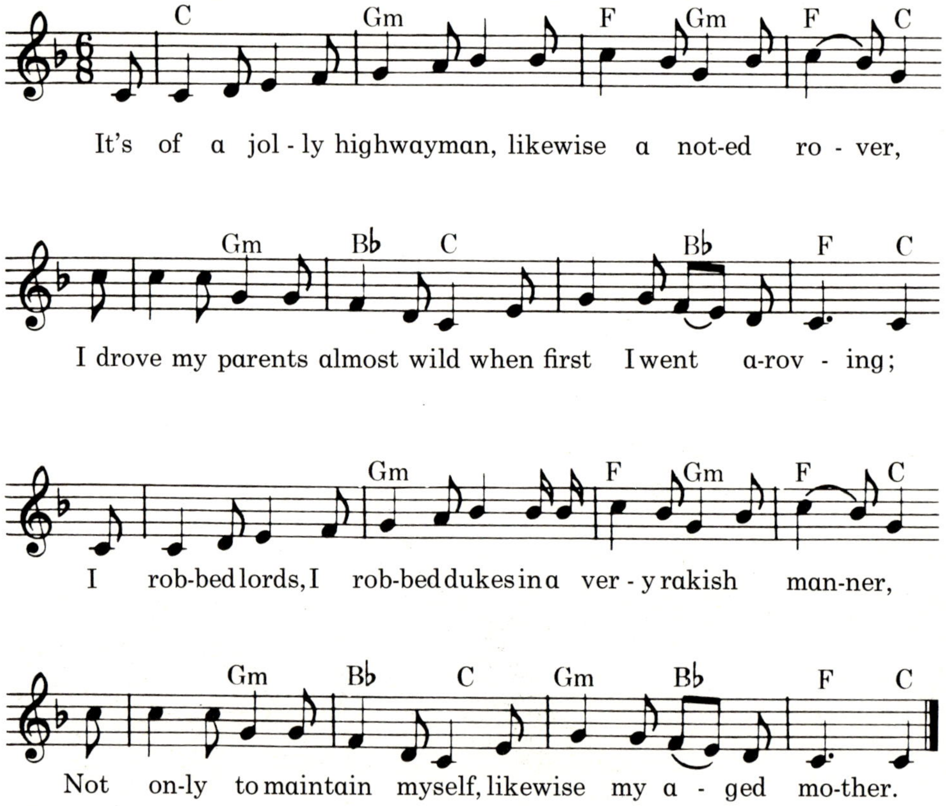

2

The very first man that I did rob, it being a lord of honour,
I did abuse that mighty lord in a very rakish manner.
"Deliver your money, my lord," said I, "without any more desire,
For if you don't it's my delight with powder and shot to fire."

3

I put a pistol to his breast which made him for to shiver,
Ten hundred guineas all in bright gold to me he did deliver,
Besides a gold repeater watch to me he did surrender,
I thought I had a noble prize for such a small endeavour.

4

The very next man that I did rob was down in Covent Garden,
And not long after he was robb'd in Newgate I was fasten'd,
To hear the turnkeys and the locks and bolts at six o'clock in the morning,
So under Newgate I must drop, so fare you well companions.

Making Music

You and your friends can sing the song on the page opposite and play the music on instruments. You could play the melody on the recorder, play the chords at the top of the music on the guitar and make sound effects too. The coconuts and yogurt pots can sound like horses' hooves, the sticks can be the ticking of the watch, the paper bag, blown up and popped can be the sound of the powder and shot and the triangle can be the jingling of money and the locks and bolts at Newgate prison too!

Ned Kelly

Ned Kelly and his gang roamed the Australian bushlands of Victoria and New South Wales from 1878 to 1880. They killed three policemen, captured two whole towns and soon became national heroes. The Kelly gang included Ned and his younger brother Dan, Joe Byrne and Steve Hart.

The Kelly family had come to Australia from Ireland. When the Irish immigrants arrived, there was no land for them to settle. All the good land had already been taken by a few people who had money. Some poorer families like the Kellys felt that some of Australia's riches should be theirs and they took to stealing horses and cattle.

Ned first got into trouble with the law when he was only 14. He and his family used to round up horses, re-brand them and sell them. The people whose horses were being stolen offered large rewards for Kelly's arrest. But no one was interested in betraying him and helping these rich men, so Kelly remained free. After the Kelly gang murdered a policeman, the police were up in arms as well. By then the Kelly gang were heroes of the poor. Poems and songs were written, and thousands of post cards said to show pictures of the gang were sold.

Finally the Kelly gang was destroyed by a large police force. The gang were holding 60 hostages inside the Glenrowan Inn. Kelly was dressed in home-made armour. It weighed 40 kg and was about 15 kg heavier and much clumsier than the armour medieval knights wore. Kelly could hardly hold up his gun to fire it. Still, Ned Kelly, who faced all the police, was the only gang member to survive the siege and burning of the inn. He had 28 bullet wounds and was badly bruised, but he recovered – only to be hanged five months later at the age of 25.

Pancho Villa

Pancho Villa lived in Mexico. He became an outlaw by accident. When Villa was only 16 he came home and found a rich and powerful man attacking his sister. Villa shot the man. The authorities then put out a warrant for his capture dead or alive.

Finally Villa was caught and sent to prison to await his execution. One day the guard took him outside to grind some corn. He began to work, and when the guard was not paying attention, Villa killed him with the grindstone. Villa ran and found a wild pony which carried him off. He went to his family who gave him food and a good horse. His life was now in great danger, and he had to flee his home town.

Then Villa was betrayed by someone he had thought was a friend. He awoke one morning in a field to find seven men standing over him with carbine rifles. Villa said he would surrender but suggested that he and the men have a meal before setting off for the prison.

The men did not know that Villa's horse was grazing 400 m away and his saddle was hidden nearby. Villa's pistol was underneath his blanket. The leader agreed to the meal and sent two of his men to gather maize and another two to gather firewood, leaving three to guard Villa. Villa grabbed his pistol and fired it at his three guards. They scrambled for cover and Villa ran for his horse. By the time the seven lawmen began to chase him, Villa was relaxing in his secret hideout.

Later in his life Villa became a great general in the Mexican revolutionary war. He fought for the rights of Mexico's poor people. In 1923, on a visit to his home town, Pancho Villa was assassinated. No one ever found out who killed him.

In later life Pancho Villa became a revolutionary general.

The Ten Guinea Highwayman

by Rosemary Border

"Your buttonholes are improving, son," Tom Pettigrew's father told him. "We'll make a tailor of you yet—which is a good thing, as Simon is leaving on Friday. Then you'll be my chief assistant—not bad for a lad of twelve, eh?"

Tom looked closely at his father, who looked more careworn than usual. "Is Simon starting his own business, then?" he asked. "We'll miss him."

"I don't know, son. I had to send him away—I couldn't afford his wages any longer."

"But father, we're doing more business than ever before. Look at the order books!"

"The customers are so slow in paying, Tom. Why, there are fathers of families who still owe me for their wedding suits!" He tried to laugh.

"That's shameful! It's as bad as stealing. Don't they know you have bills to pay too?"

"Don't talk to me about bills, son," said John Pettigrew. "I owe money for cloth, and buttons, and I don't know what else. It's getting bad, really bad. If I can't pay my bills, it's the Debtor's Prison for me!"

Tom shuddered. Once people went there, they stayed there until their debts were paid. Some people died there; and their families—well, it was better not to think about them.

"It's unjust!" Tom burst out. "What about the rich folk who owe you money? Why don't they go to prison until they pay you?"

"They're rich, son, and money means power. It's the little men like us who suffer... Tom, Tom, I'm at my wits' end. I dare not tell your mother, but unless I can find ten guineas by next week, old Bates the cloth merchant will have the bailiffs on us!"

Tom knew about bailiffs. They had the right to enter a man's home, search it for anything of value, and seize that in payment of the debt. Nothing, and nobody, was safe from them. It would break his mother's heart.

That night Tom sat up late, embroidering some cuffs and worrying about his father. Suddenly he pushed

the fine work aside, rubbed his tired eyes and went to the cupboard where his father kept the account book.

Holding the page close to the lamp, Tom read the whole sad story. John Pettigrew had dressed the greatest men in the county. Many a fine gentleman danced at the county ball in clothes for which he had not paid.

"Sir Matthew Huntley," Tom read, "ten guineas... why, he's owed that for over a year. Yet he reads the lesson in church as if he had nothing on his conscience! AND he's a magistrate... he's probably sent men to prison, or even the gallows, for less than he owes my father! 'Justice of the Peace' indeed! Where's the justice in that?"

The next day officials came around, posting handbills. A highwayman was at large in the area. Citizens were to watch out for a man on a bay mare, armed with a brace of pistols.

"Take care when you ride out to deliver that order, Tom," said his father.

"I've nothing to steal," laughed Tom. "If he finds any money on me, we'll share it!" And so Tom's great idea was born. He would hold up Sir Matthew's carriage and take the ten guineas. As Tom stitched away at his buttonholes, the plan took shape.

His father's old pistol, sneaked out of the drawer where it was kept in case of thieves... his own old horse.. There were black cloaks in the shop... a mask? Tom sat up late making one from some black silk, left over from Lord Wilberforce's waistcoat. His own high boots, which he wore against the whistling draughts of their chilly workroom, completed the outfit.

The whole county knew that Sir Matthew went to the nearby town every Thursday, on business. He set out from Huntley Hall in his carriage, returning between six and half past, in time to change for dinner.

"He'll be a little late for dinner!" thought Tom grimly.

Sir Matthew Huntley and Arabella, his only daughter and the apple of her father's eye, were lurching homeward in their carriage.

"Damned mud!" said Sir Matthew crossly, "they should do something about these roads.... Did you have a good time in town, my dear?" Before Arabella could reply, the carriage stopped suddenly. Sir Matthew stuck his head out of the window.

"Coachman, what's happening?" he bellowed. Soon it became all too clear. Ahead of them, black against the twilight sky, was a tall, slender figure on horseback, masked and cloaked and armed with a pistol. On his feet were high leather boots.

"A highwayman!" breathed Arabella. "How exciting!"

"Please climb out, Sir Matthew," the highwayman said in a deep, unnatural voice. "Coachman, please drive on. I do not wish this young lady to be a part of such a distressing scene. Her mother will be anxious." He bowed to the delighted Arabella. The coachman hesitated a moment, then, at a word from Sir Matthew drove away, leaving his master ankle-deep in mud.

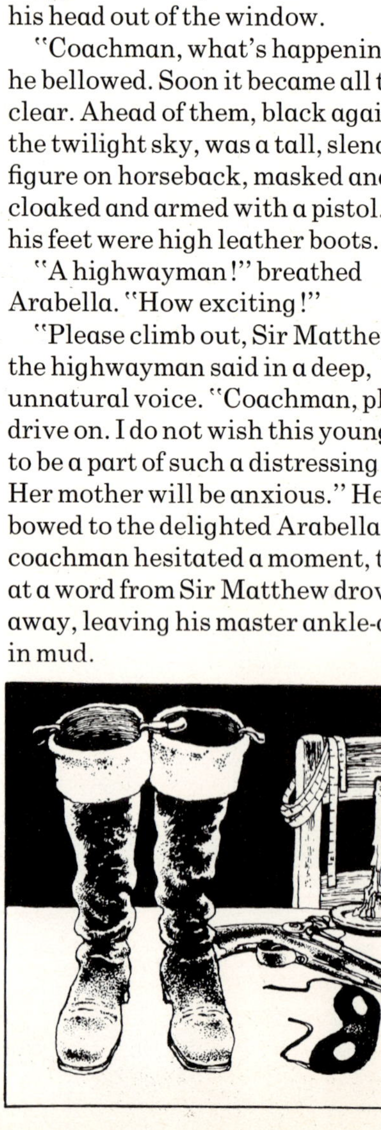

("Cunning rogue," thought Sir Matthew, "He wants to disguise his voice!")

"Your purse, sir," said the highwayman. He extracted ten guineas and tossed the rest back to Sir Matthew. "That is enough," he said, "I am not a greedy man. Now, Sir, you are free to go. It is only four miles —some of your tenants walk it twice a day, in worse weather than this!" And he rode away, leaving his victim to stumble along the dark road under a steady rain. The highwayman dodged behind some bushes and became Tom Pettigrew, out delivering an order.

At supper that night, Tom gave his father the ten guineas.

"You can tell Mr Bates what to do with his bailiffs!" he said. "Sir Matthew Huntley paid his bill while you were out."

John Pettigrew ran to enter the payment in the book. "It couldn't have come at a better time!" he said. Tom just smiled.

In the morning John Pettigrew looked up to see Sir Matthew and Miss Arabella entering the shop. "Tom!" he called, "Bring chairs! We have important customers!"

Tom ran in from the chilly workroom, saw the visitors, and waited for the heavens to fall.

"Ah, Pettigrew," said Sir Matthew, "I have some work for you. A highwayman robbed me last night. He sent my carriage on, with Miss Arabella . . . showed a fine regard for her feelings, but precious little for my clothes! He sent me home on foot, the blackguard, and my suit is ruined!"

Miss Arabella tried to hide a smile. "So I want you to make me a new one, Pettigrew . . . by the way, I believe I owe you money?"

"Why no, Sir Matthew," said the tailor. "Tom—the book. You see, sir— 'Paid With Thanks'."

Just then Arabella looked at Tom's boots. "Father," she said, "Look, those boots are just like the highwayman's!"

"Stuff and nonsense," began her father. Then he saw Tom's terrified face.

"Great thunder!" he shouted. "Guilt written all over you! Well, what have you to say for yourself before I turn you over to the law? You cut a pretty dashing figure last night —I warrant you'll look well at the end of a rope!"

"There must be some mistake," began John Pettigrew.

"No, Father," said Tom, "there's no mistake." He looked the wealthy man straight in the eye. "I took ten guineas from this—gentleman, ten guineas that he had owed you for more than a year, while he and others like him sent poor, desperate souls to the gallows for less. Justice of the Peace— ha!" He went on, "And if I hadn't gone out and got that money, you'd have been in the Debtor's Prison by now— all because men like this do not pay their bills to honest tradesmen who serve them well!"

Sir Matthew's face was like a thundercloud. But Arabella laid her hand on his arm. "Father," she said, "if you were in the same position as poor Mr Pettigrew, I should do just the same as his son has done! And really, Father, is it right of you to be so lax about your bills? How would you feel if someone went to prison because of your absent-mindedness? . . . No, I will not be quiet! I shall tell everybody about you unless you promise to pardon this boy, and pay all your other bills!"

"You've had too much of your own way, Arabella," her father growled. . . . "Oh, very well." He turned to Tom. "Did you realize that you could have gone to prison, even the gallows, for what you did?"

"Yes, Sir. But it was that, or letting my father be ruined through no fault of his own. Could you stand by if it was your father, Sir?"

Sir Matthew flushed and looked away. Then he turned to John Pettigrew. "I want your boy to make me two suits, with fine-stitched buttonholes and embroidered lapels. That will keep him off the highways for some time to come! And here is half payment in advance. Come, Arabella."

This time, Miss Arabella made no effort to hide her smile.

Bonnie and Clyde

Bonnie Parker and Clyde Barrow were on the list of the ten most wanted criminals in the south-west United States. They robbed and murdered for two violent years before they were finally caught. Bonnie was only 19 and Clyde 21 when they first met.

In the 1930's people in America were very poor, but Bonnie and Clyde still took what little these people had. They usually raided petrol stations and small shops. Sometimes Clyde's brother and his wife or another friend came along to help by driving the getaway car. If the Barrow gang needed another car, they stole it.

When the gang had enough money, they set off on a motoring trip. They stayed at grand hotels, ate at expensive restaurants and bought new clothes. Bonnie and Clyde always tried to look smart.

When they ran out of money, the gang began to rob and kill again. Bonnie also wrote poems and sent them to newspapers where they were printed. Despite their horrible deeds Bonnie and Clyde became popular heroes.

The police from four states were after them. It seemed that every police officer who got too close to them was killed. Once when Bonnie and Clyde became homesick they went back to Texas and met their mothers in an abandoned quarry to have a picnic. Then they were on the run again.

The police finally caught up with them. They were ambushed and 167 shots were fired into their car. Even after that, the police were afraid that Bonnie and Clyde might not really be dead. But they had died—with their guns still in their hands.

Some Lawmen

At the time when highwaymen were operating, there was no real police force in England. The government offered rewards for bringing criminals to justice. The people who lived by catching criminals were called thief-takers. Their reward was £40 as well as the highwayman's horse, money and weapons. Most thief-takers were criminals themselves who betrayed their friends for the reward called "blood-money".

In 1749 Henry Fielding, with the help of his brother John, set up a small detective force called the Bow Street Runners. The six runners were given this name because Fielding's office was in Bow Street in London. The Bow Street Runners soon had a horse patrol too. They did such a good job that by 1764 the highwaymen were gone and the roads leading from London were safe. The government then decided that the patrol was no longer needed. But once the patrol was gone, the highwaymen returned, and even the Prime Minister was robbed! It was not until the last century that England finally had a proper police force.

Henry Fielding, the magistrate, was also a great novelist.

John Fielding continued at Bow Street after his brother Henry died.

The Bow Street Office in 1750.

American lawmen in the 1880's.

Life was very dangerous in the western United States 100 years ago when Jesse James and his kind were robbing and killing. At first the only real law was the law of the gun. Often the only peace keepers were gunslingers, saloon keepers and gamblers—almost criminals themselves. Eventually because of their skill with guns they were accepted as officers of the law—sheriffs and marshals. They had small police forces, made up of ordinary citizens. These were led by U.S. Marshals, each appointed by the President of the United States.

Besides the government lawmen, there were also private detective agencies. The most famous of these was Pinkerton's. In the 1860's Allan Pinkerton and his men began to track down criminals that even the government could not catch. The old Pinkerton trade mark was a picture of an open eye with the slogan "we never sleep". This is why detectives are sometimes called "private eyes". The Pinkerton Agency has survived to this day. It is now the largest detective agency in the world.

A U.S. Marshal's badge.

Allan Pinkerton began the famous Pinkerton's Detective Agency.

Who Did What?

1. Who wore this at Glenrowan?

2. Who was a farmer by day and a highwayman by night?

3. Who charmed women he robbed?

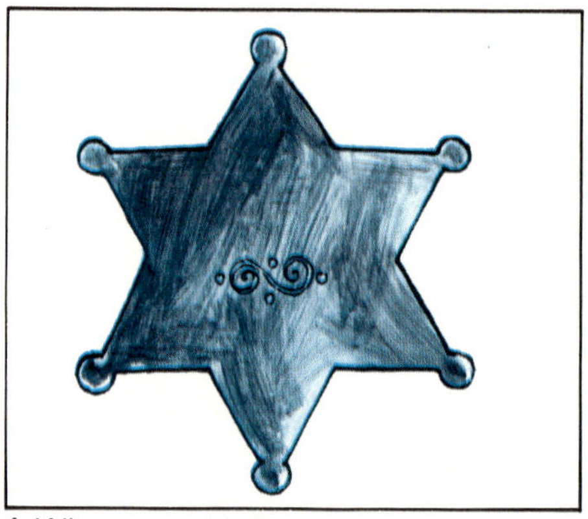

4. Who wore this?

5. Who bowed to the crowds as he was taken here?

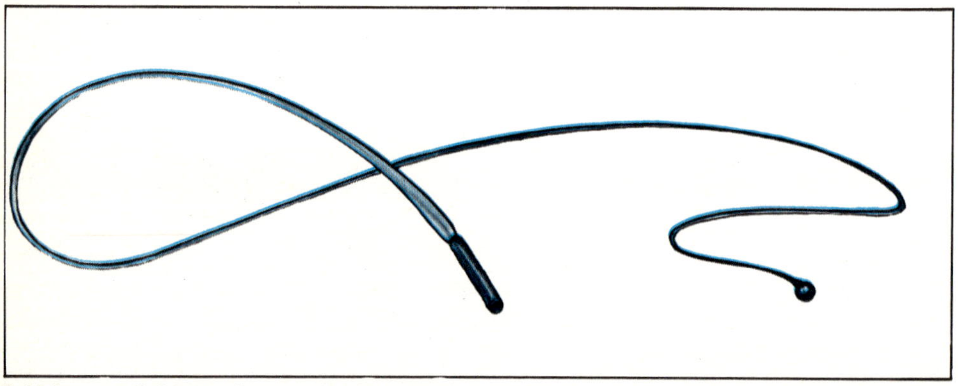

6. Who used this and what did he steal?

See page 47 for the answers.

7. Who robbed these and how did they do it?

8. Besides writing novels, what did he do?

9. Who is she and who loved her?

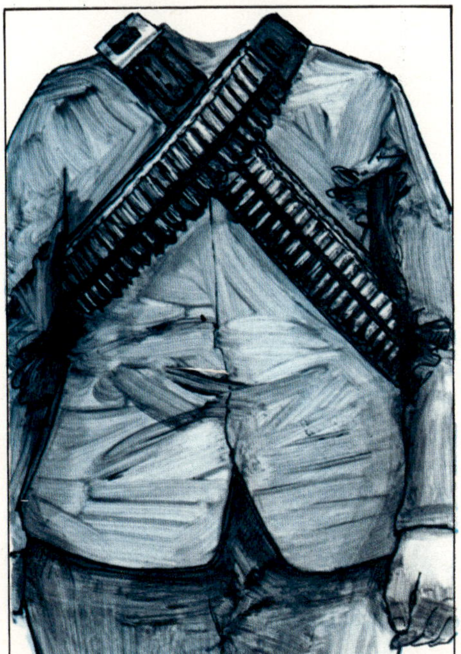

10. Who wore this and what was he besides a bandit?

11. Who was given this?

12. Which bandit couple stole cars and always looked smart?

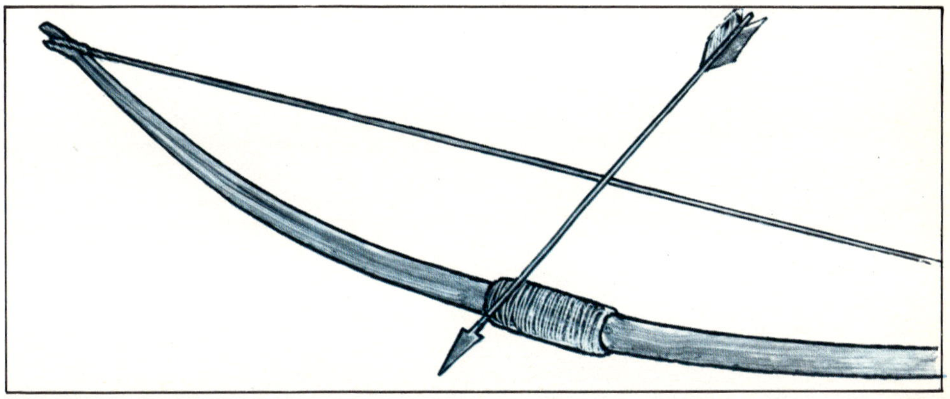

13. Who was an expert with this?

Did You Know?

Highwaymen in the 1720's in London were known to fix up notices on the doors of rich people's houses forbidding them to go out without at least ten guineas and a gold watch on them, upon pain of death!

The highwayman Jack Sheppard was not a very successful robber, but he was very good at breaking out of prison. He was small and could slip through the bars. Once he was helped to escape from Newgate prison by two women called Edgworth Bess and Poll Maggot. Sheppard was handsome and witty and very popular in London. Within months of his execution at the age of 22, more than ten versions of his life story were published.

In the 18th century printers sometimes gave out tickets to public executions. They were meant as jokes to advertise for business, but anyone could come to a hanging in a large place like Tyburn and outside Newgate prison. In the western United States in the 19th century real invitations were sent out for executions. These were used as tickets to get into the prison yards.

In the 17th and 18th centuries criminals, including highwaymen, were often gibbeted after they were hanged. Their bodies were taken down from the gallows and put into irons and displayed in a public place like a busy road. This ghastly sight was supposed to frighten other criminals into reforming.